by Iain Gray

LangSyne
PUBLISHING
WRITING *to* REMEMBER

Lang**Syne**
PUBLISHING
WRITING *to* REMEMBER

79 Main Street, Newtongrange,
Midlothian EH22 4NA
Tel: 0131 344 0414   Fax: 0845 075 6085
E-mail: info@lang-syne.co.uk
www.langsyneshop.co.uk

Design by Dorothy Meikle
Printed by Printwell Ltd
© Lang Syne Publishers Ltd 2019

All rights reserved. No part of this publication may be reproduced, stored or introduced into a retrieval system, or transmitted in any form or by any means (electronic, mechanical, photocopying, recording or otherwise) without the prior written permission of Lang Syne Publishers Ltd.

ISBN 978-1-85217-473-6

Rae

MOTTO:
Ready for everything.

CREST:
A stag.

TERRITORY:
The Borders, present-day Dumfries and Galloway and the Highlands.

NAME variations include:
  Ray
  Raith
  Reay
  Macrae *(Gaelic)*

*The spirit of the clan means
much to thousands of people*

Chapter one:

The origins of the clan system

by Rennie McOwan

The original Scottish clans of the Highlands and the great families of the Lowlands and Borders were gatherings of families, relatives, allies and neighbours for mutual protection against rivals or invaders.

Scotland experienced invasion from the Vikings, the Romans and English armies from the south. The Norman invasion of what is now England also had an influence on land-holding in Scotland. Some of these invaders stayed on and in time became 'Scottish'.

The word clan derives from the Gaelic language term 'clann', meaning children, and it was first used many centuries ago as communities were formed around tribal lands in glens and mountain fastnesses.

The format of clans changed over the centuries, but at its best the chief and his family held the land on behalf of all, like trustees, and the ordinary clansmen and women believed they had a blood relationship with the founder of their clan.

There were two way duties and obligations. An inadequate chief could be deposed and replaced by someone of greater ability.

Clan people had an immense pride in race. Their relationship with the chief was like adult children to a father and they had a real dignity.

The concept of clanship is very old and a more feudal notion of authority gradually crept in.

Pictland, for instance, was divided into seven principalities ruled by feudal leaders who were the strongest and most charismatic leaders of their particular groups.

By the sixth century the 'British' kingdoms of Strathclyde, Lothian and Celtic Dalriada (Argyll) had emerged and Scotland, as one nation, began to take shape in the time of King Kenneth MacAlpin.

Some chiefs claimed descent from ancient kings which may not have been accurate in every case.

By the twelfth and thirteenth centuries the clans and families were more strongly brought under the central control of Scottish monarchs.

Lands were awarded and administered more and more under royal favour, yet the power of the area clan chiefs was still very great.

The long wars to ensure Scotland's

independence against the expansionist ideas of English monarchs extended the influence of some clans and reduced the lands of others.

Those who supported Scotland's greatest king, Robert the Bruce, were awarded the territories of the families who had opposed his claim to the Scottish throne.

In the Scottish Borders country – the notorious Debatable Lands – the great families built up a ferocious reputation for providing warlike men accustomed to raiding into England and occasionally fighting one another.

Chiefs had the power to dispense justice and to confiscate lands and clan warfare produced a society where martial virtues – courage, hardiness, tenacity – were greatly admired.

Gradually the relationship between the clans and the Crown became strained as Scottish monarchs became more orientated to life in the Lowlands and, on occasion, towards England.

The Highland clans spoke a different language, Gaelic, whereas the language of Lowland Scotland and the court was Scots and in more modern times, English.

Highlanders dressed differently, had different

customs, and their wild mountain land sometimes seemed almost foreign to people living in the Lowlands.

It must be emphasised that Gaelic culture was very rich and story-telling, poetry, piping, the clarsach (harp) and other music all flourished and were greatly respected.

Highland culture was different from other parts of Scotland but it was not inferior or less sophisticated.

Central Government, whether in London or Edinburgh, sometimes saw the Gaelic clans as a challenge to their authority and some sent expeditions into the Highlands and west to crush the power of the Lords of the Isles.

Nevertheless, when the eighteenth century Jacobite Risings came along the cause of the Stuarts was mainly supported by Highland clans.

The word Jacobite comes from the Latin for James – Jacobus. The Jacobites wanted to restore the exiled Stuarts to the throne of Britain.

The monarchies of Scotland and England became one in 1603 when King James VI of Scotland (1st of England) gained the English throne after Queen Elizabeth died.

The Union of Parliaments of Scotland and England, the Treaty of Union, took place in 1707.

Some Highland clans, of course, and Lowland families opposed the Jacobites and supported the incoming Hanoverians.

After the Jacobite cause finally went down at Culloden in 1746 a kind of ethnic cleansing took place. The power of the chiefs was curtailed. Tartan and the pipes were banned in law.

Many emigrated, some because they wanted to, some because they were evicted by force. In addition, many Highlanders left for the cities of the south to seek work.

Many of the clan lands became home to sheep and deer shooting estates.

But the warlike traditions of the clans and the great Lowland and Border families lived on, with their descendants fighting bravely for freedom in two world wars.

Remember the men from whence you came, says the Gaelic proverb, and to that could be added the role of many heroic women.

The spirit of the clan, of having roots, whether Highland or Lowland, means much to thousands of people.

The origins of the clan system

Clan warfare produced a society where courage and tenacity were greatly admired

Chapter two:

Highland and Lowland

A name with a number of spelling variants that include Ray and Rea, bearers of the Rae name appear in Scotland's historical record from the earliest times.

In the now redundant forms of Raa and Ra, a Robert Raa is recorded in Culross, Fife, in 1231, while further west Thomas Ra is recorded in Glasgow in 1281.

Although to be found all over Scotland, the largest concentration of the name was in the Borders and present-day Dumfries and Galloway, while in the Gaelic form of Macrae another main territory was the far-flung Highlands.

The actual roots of the name are buried in the dim and distant past, but one suggestion is that it may derive from 'roe', as in roe deer and, in common with this animal, denoting a timid nature.

Another possibility is that it is a location surname, with one source pointing out the presence of the ancient settlement of Wrae, in the present-day Borders area of Tweeddale.

The Gaelic version 'Macrae', meanwhile, derives from *Mac-Rath*, meaning 'son of grace' or 'son of prosperity.'

Complicating matters somewhat, a common form of the Rae name is Reay and, in this form, may well derive from the village of Reay, about 12 miles west of Thurso in Caithness.

'Lord Reay', meanwhile, is not only a title in the Peerage of the United Kingdom but also – according to local folklore – the name of a magician.

The title of Lord Reay, of Reay in the County of Caithness, was created in 1628 for Sir Donald Mackay while the holder of the title at the time of writing is Hugh William Mackay, 14th Lord Reay.

It is at some period in the distant past that the magician known as Lord Reay is reputed to have engaged in a magical contest with a witch who lived in a cave.

Lord Reay was triumphant and, as his prize, was given control of a band of fairies whose only desire was to work as hard as possible.

Lord Reay set them the task of building a number of earthworks throughout the parish of Reay, but even this could not satisfy their voracious appetite for work.

Having completed the earthworks, he then set them the task of building a causeway of sand across the Pentland Firth.

This has kept them happily occupied ever since – because the currents wash away the sand as fast as the fairies can toil.

Although, as noted, the Rae name may have originally denoted someone of a timid nature, this was certainly not an apt description of the vast majority of bearers of the name.

One historical source describes them as having been 'a troublesome Border clan' – something of an understatement considering the state of near anarchy in which some families existed for centuries in the wild Border area.

A Privy Council report of 1608 graphically described how the 'wild incests, adulteries, convocation of the lieges, shooting and wearing of hackbuts, pistols, lances, daily bloodshed, oppression, and disobedience in civil matters, neither are nor has been punished.'

A constant thorn in the flesh of both the English and Scottish authorities was the cross-border raiding and pillaging carried out by well-mounted and heavily armed men, the contingent from the

Scottish side of the border known and feared as 'moss troopers.'

In an attempt to bring order to what was known as the wild 'debateable land' on both sides of the border, Alexander II of Scotland had in 1237 signed the Treaty of York, which for the first time established the Scottish border with England as a line running from the Solway to the Tweed.

On either side of the border there were three 'marches' or areas of administration, the West, East and Middle Marches, and a warden governed these.

Complaints from either side of the border were dealt with on Truce Days, when the wardens of the different marches would act as arbitrators.

There was also a law known as the Hot Trod, that granted anyone who had their livestock stolen the right to pursue the thieves and recover their property.

It was following the Union of the Crowns in 1603 that James I (James VI of Scotland) attempted to crush the Border mayhem once and for all.

The very term 'Borders' was abolished and renamed 'the Middle Shires', while scores of particularly unruly families were forcibly uprooted and either conscripted into military service or banished to Ireland.

While 'Reay' is a recognised spelling variant of 'Ray', somewhat confusingly the Reays are recognised as a sept, or sub-branch, of Clan Mackay, whose motto is *With a strong hand* and crest a dagger held erect.

The Raes, however, are a sept of the equally distinguished but wholly separate Clan Macrae – whose proud motto is *With fortitude* and crest an arm with the hand grasping a sword.

Sharing a common ancestry with both the Mackenzies and the Macleans, the main territory of the clan, in whose fortunes and misfortunes bearers of the Rae named shared, was the Kintail area of the Western Highlands.

In common with their namesakes in the Scottish Borders, they also frequently suffered from the wrath of the Crown.

Chapter three:

Fire and sword

In 1568, James VI expressed his contempt for his wild and unruly subjects in the far-flung Highlands and Islands when he wrote: "As for the Highlands, I shortly comprehend them all in two sorts of people.

"The one that dwelleth in our main land, that are barbarous for the most part, and yet mixed with some show of civility: the other, that dwelleth in the isles, that are utterly barbarous, without any sort of show of civility."

It was during the reign of James VI that in 1597 an Act of Parliament was passed to suppress what was considered to be the 'barbarous inhumanity' of Highlanders and Islanders.

The monarch, certainly no friend of his far flung western seaboard and northern subjects, accordingly issued what were known as *Letters of Fire and Sword* to bring the unruly clansmen such as the Macraes and their kinsfolk such as the Raes to heel.

In what became known as the Daunting of the Isles, the Isle of Lewis was signalled out for special attention in a campaign that would today be described as ethnic cleansing.

Seeking to justify the savage attack to be launched on the islanders, the Privy Council condemned 'the beastly and monstrous cruelties' that the islanders inflicted upon one another, and pointed out that the rich and fertile lands of Lewis would be better managed by others.

The unruly Lewismen, the Privy Council complained, were possessed with 'the most fertile and commodious part of the whole realm ... being enriched with incredible fertility of corns and plenty of fish.'

Accordingly, in 1598, James VI issued a charter, or contract, to a band of speculators who became known as the Fife Adventurers, because it was from Fife that the majority of them hailed.

Backed by a 600-strong force of mercenaries led by the Duke of Lennox, the adventurers attempted to wipe out the inhabitants of Lewis and take their lands for themselves.

They received a rude shock, however, when a hardy band of inhabitants led by Neil Macleod, a brother of a Macleod Clan Chief, fought back with such ferocity that the dismayed mercenaries described them as 'barbarous, bloody, and wicked Hielandmen.'

One of the Fife Adventurers was captured and ransomed, only to die from the privations he had suffered during his captivity.

The adventurers withdrew and another force was later sent to renew the attempt at bringing the clansmen to heel, but this also proved abortive.

Further desperate attempts were made to stamp the authority of the Crown on the Highlands and Islands through the Statutes of Iona of 1609 and parallel legislation in 1616.

Bards were to be treated in the same manner as beggars, and likely to have their ears cut off and banished – facing death by hanging if they returned.

Attempts were also made to replace the Gaelic language with English and the translation of the Bible into Gaelic was banned. It was also required that the eldest son or daughter of every clan chief or 'gentleman' who owned goods worth 60 cattle or more should be educated in the Lowlands.

An attempt was also made to 'plant' Lowland cultivators on the lands of those chiefs who failed to produce written proof of the right to hold their lands – this proved disastrous, however, and the scheme was abandoned.

Strict controls were enforced on the distilling

of whisky to prevent its illegal sale; the ordinary man was allowed to distil whisky, but only in his own home and for his own use.

As kinsfolk of the Macraes, the Raes were also to be frequently found on the bloody field of battle.

Following the flight into exile of the Stuart monarch James II (James VII of Scotland) in 1688, the Protestant William of Orange and his wife Mary succeeded to the throne.

Jacobites, as supporters of the exiled Royal House of Stuart were known, raised the banner of revolt in 1715 following the succession to the throne of George, the Elector of Hanover. One of the main leaders of the revolt, John Erskine, 6th Earl of Mar, raised the Stuart Standard at Braemar.

But, plagued by bad leadership and squabbles over what military strategy to adopt, the Jacobite campaign was doomed almost from the start.

The cause was effectively lost following the battle of Sheriffmuir, near Dunblane, in November, when Mar lost the initiative against the Hanoverian forces led by John Campbell, 2nd Duke of Argyll, by withdrawing to Perth.

Among the many Jacobite dead at Sheriffmuir were more than 60 Macraes and their kinsfolk.

Nearly four years later, the Macraes and their kinsfolk were involved in yet another sad drama concerning the Royal House of Stuart.

Situated on a small island in Loch Duich, in the Western Highlands, is Eilean Donan Castle – of which the Macraes had become hereditary constables, through their role as 'protectors' of the Mackenzies, in 1511.

It was here than an advance party of 300 Spanish troops arrived in April of 1719 to lend support for what would prove to be yet another doomed Jacobite Rising.

A fleet of Royal navy ships arrived in the loch a few weeks later and, subjecting the castle to a furious bombardment, soon battered the garrison into submission.

The castle was then methodically destroyed stone by ancient stone by charges of gunpowder – and was not rebuilt until between 1919 and 1932 by Lieutenant Colonel John MacRae-Gilstrap.

The home today of Clan Macrae, it is also a popular venue for a host of events.

In later centuries and on much different fields of battle, bearers of the Rae name – in all its rich variety of spellings – have gained honour.

Born in 1872 in Pensacola, North Carolina, Charles W. Ray was a late nineteenth century recipient of the Medal of Honor – America's highest award for military valour.

He had been a sergeant in the United States Army during the Philippine-American War of 1899 to 1902 when near Luzon, on the Philippine Islands, in October of 1899 he led a detachment that captured and held a vital bridge crossing; he died in 1959.

A high-ranking Canadian Army soldier of the late twentieth century, Lieutenant General Gordon Reay, more familiarly known as Gord Reay, was born in 1943 in Royston, Hertfordshire.

Emigrating from England to Canada with his family as a child and later graduating from the Royal Military College of Canada, he went on to hold a number of senior command posts that include Commanding Officer of 1st Battalion Princess Patricia's Canadian Light Infantry and, in 1993, Chief of the Land Staff of the Canadian Forces.

He was killed in a road accident in December of 2000 while on a humanitarian mission in Croatia.

From the battlefield to the world of academia and the sciences, bearers of the name have also stamped their mark on the historical record.

Not only an academic but also a clergyman, Stephen Reay was born in 1782 in Montrose, Angus.

Graduating from Edinburgh University in his native Scotland in 1802 and ordained four years later in Chester Cathedral, England, he was appointed Laudian Professor of Arabic at Oxford University in 1840. Also in charge of the collection of oriental books at the university's famed Bodleian Library, he died in 1861.

In one of the original Rae homelands of Scotland, John Rae, born in 1845 and who died in 1915, was the journalist and writer known for his biography of the Scottish economist Adam Smith, *Life of Adam Smith*.

Influenced by the work of fellow Scot Adam Smith and sharing the same name as his biographer, John Rae was the Scots-Canadian economist born in 1796 in Footdee, Aberdeenshire.

Later immigrating to Canada, he became famous before his death in 1872 for pioneering works on economic theory that include *Statement of Some New Principles on the Subject of Political Economy*.

Another Scot-born bearer of the Rae name had a significant impact on the early history of labour relations in the United States.

This was the coal miner John B. Rae, who was aged 37 when he immigrated with his wife and four children to America, settling in Westmoreland County, Pennsylvania.

It was along with John McBride that in 1890 he co-founded the United Mine Workers of America, serving as its first president; he died in 1922.

One particularly far-travelled and intrepid Scottish bearer of the Rae name was the medical doctor and explorer John Rae, born in 1813 at Hall of Clestrain, in the Orkney parish of Orphir.

Qualifying as a doctor in 1833 after studying medicine at Edinburgh, he gained employment with the Hudson's Bay Company, working as a surgeon for nearly a decade at Moose Factory, Ontario.

He became respected not only for his medical skills but also for his extraordinary stamina – taking off on frequent expeditions and living off the land like the indigenous population, the Inuit.

From 1844 to 1845, wanting to learn the skills of surveying, he embarked on an arduous 1,200 mile trek through snow-covered forests – earning him the Inuit nickname of *Aglooka* – 'he who takes long strides.'

In 1848, along with Sir John Richardson, he embarked on a search for the elusive Northwest

Passage – a task in which the pair and their team eventually succeeded.

This was to find a sea route through the Arctic Ocean, along the northern coast of North America, connecting the Atlantic and Pacific Oceans.

But controversy came in 1859 when, while exploring the Boothia Peninsula, the local Inuit furnished him with disturbing information regarding the mysterious disappearance of the Franklin Naval Expedition – that had set off in in its own search for the Northwest Passage.

Rae reported to the British Admiralty that the doomed expedition had been forced to resort to cannibalism at one stage – a claim that caused shock and outrage in Britain.

It was largely for this reason that Rae, in his lifetime, never received the recognition he justly deserved for his own role in finding the Northwest Passage.

In 1860, he was again on his travels – this time helping to carry out the survey for a telegraph line between Canada and America.

Later returning to Britain he died in London, aged 80 – and was interred in the kirkyard of St Magnus' Cathedral, in his native Orkney.

Chapter four:

On the world stage

Bearers of the Rae name, in a variety of its spellings, have gained international acclaim.

Born Corinne Jacqueline Bailey in Leeds in 1979, **Corinne Bailey Rae** is the award-winning singer, songwriter and guitarist who studied classical violin before embarking on a career as a singer.

Married to Jason Rae from 2001 until the Scottish musician's death in 2008, her best-selling album *The Sea* was nominated for the 2010 Mercury Music Prize for Album of the Year.

The recipient of a star on the Hollywood Walk of Fame, **Johnnie Ray** was the American singer, songwriter and pianist born John Alvin Ray in Dallas, Oregon, in 1927.

An accident at the age of 13 left him deaf in one ear, while surgery carried out in 1958 in a bid to rectify this left him almost completely deaf.

Before this, he had major hits that include the 1951 *Whiskey and Gin*, the 1954 *Alexander's Ragtime Band* and, from 1956, *Who's Sorry Now*.

Following his abortive surgery, and with the

help of hearing aids, he enjoyed further chart success with songs that include the 1961 *Shop Around*.

He died in 1990, having also appeared in films that include the 1954 *There's No Business Like Showbusiness* and the 1968 *Rogue's Gallery*.

In contemporary music, **Chris Rea**, born in 1951 in Middlesbrough, is the English singer and songwriter whose hits include *The Road to Hell (Part 2)* and the 1978 *Fool (If You Think It's Over)*, later covered by Elkie Brooks.

Best known for his work as a guitarist with Paul McCartney, **Brian Ray** is the American session musician, singer and songwriter born in California in 1955.

In addition to working with the former Beatle on albums that include *Memory Almost Full* and *Back in the World*, he has also collaborated with other artists who include Bo Diddley and Joe Cocker.

Bearers of the Rae name, in all its rich variety of spellings, have also excelled in the highly competitive world of sport.

On the fields of European football, **Robin Rae** is the Scottish former goalkeeper who played for teams that include Hibernian, Hamilton and Berwick.

Born in 1964 in Musselburgh, he was also a

member of the Scotland team that won the 1982 European Under-19 Championship.

Having played for teams that include Dundee, Rangers, Cardiff City and Aberdeen, **Gavin Rae** is the Scottish midfielder and internationalist born in 1977 in Aberdeen.

Still on the fields of European football, **Alex Rae**, born in Glasgow in 1946, is the Scottish former player and manager who played for teams that include East Fife, Bury and Partick Thistle and who managed Forfar Athletic between 1980 and 1983.

Born in Glasgow in 1969, **Alexander Rae** is the Scottish footballer who, after a youth career with Rangers, played for teams that include Rangers and Falkirk and also managed Dundee from 2006 to 2008.

From football to the Canadian national sport of ice hockey, **Billy Reay** was the leading National Hockey League (NHL) player who played for ten seasons with the Montreal Canadiens and the Detroit Red Bulls.

Born in 1918 in Winnipeg, he was the winner of two prestigious Stanley Cups with the Montreal Canadiens, in 1946 and 1953.

Head coach of the Toronto Maple Leafs from

1957 to 1959 and of the Chicago Black Hawks from 1963 to 1977, he died in 2004.

Also in ice hockey, **Ronny Ray**, born in 1968 in Stirling, Ontario, is the sports broadcaster and former player for the Buffalo Sabres and Ottawa Senators who, in 1999, was awarded the King Clancy Memorial Trophy by the NHL for his leadership and humanitarianism.

In field hockey, **Cath Rae**, born in 1985 in Aberdeen, is the goalkeeper who, as a member of the Scottish national team, was awarded the title of Goalkeeper of the Tournament at both the 2001 Under-16 Championships and the 2004 Under-21 European Championship.

In snooker, **Jackie Rea** is the Northern Irish retired player born in 1921 in Dunganno, Co. Tyrone. Winner of the All-Ireland Snooker Championship and also the Northern Irish Snooker Championship in 1947, he held the title of Irish Professional Champion from 1952 until defeated by Alex Higgins in 1972.

Also in snooker, **John Rea**, born in 1951, is the Scottish retired player who won the 1989 Scottish Professional Championship.

From sport to the stage, **Nelson Rae**, born in 1915 in New Jersey, was the American actor of radio and stage who was one of the original cast of the 1940 Broadway musical *Pal Joey*, starring Gene Kelly.

Joining the U.S. Army after America's entry into the Second World War and attached to the 2nd Division Counter Intelligence Corps, he was killed in action in Belgium in 1945.

In contemporary acting, **Stephen Rea**, born in Belfast in 1946, is the Northern Irish actor of stage and film who was nominated for an Academy Award for Best Actor for his role in the 1992 film *The Crying Game*.

Other film credits include the 1970 *Cry of the Banshee*, the 1995 *Michael Collins* and, from 2004, *Breakfast on Pluto*.

Born Charlotte Ray Lubotsky in Milwaukee, Wisconsin, in 1926, **Charlotte Ray** is the multi-talented actress, comedian, singer and dancer best known for her roles in the popular American television sitcoms of the 1960s and 1970s *Diff'rent Strokes* and *The Facts of Life*.

An actor, dancer and choreographer, **Gene Ray**, born in Harlem, New York in 1962 and who died in 2003, was best known for his role as the dancer Leroy Johnson in the 1980 film *Fame* and also in the television series of the name.

Ironically, he had attended the New York High School of the Performing Arts, which inspired *Fame*, but was thrown out after only a year because of his indiscipline.

A popular British radio and television comedian and personality from the 1950s until his death in 1977, Charlie Olden, born in 1905 in Wigan, Lancashire, was much better known as **Ted Ray**.

Host of his own radio show, *Ray's A Laugh* on BBC radio from 1949 until 1961, he also appeared on the comedy radio panel *Does the Team Think?*

He was the father of the actor **Andrew Ray**, born in London in 1939 and who died in 2003.

Cast in the title part at the age of only ten in the film *The Mudlark*, also starring Alec Guinness and Irene Dunne, he subsequently appeared in a number of other films that include the 1962 *Twice Round the Daffodils* and television series that include the 1978 *Edward and Mrs Simpson*, *Upstairs, Downstairs*, *Inspector Morse* and *Peak Practice*.

A leading American film actor from the early 1950s until his death in 1991, **Aldo Ray** was born Aldo Dare in 1926 in Argyll, Pennsylvania.

Serving as a naval frogman during the Second World War and seeing action in the Pacific, it was only by chance that he later took up acting as a career. Taking a day off from his duties as a policeman, his career path altered dramatically after he drove his brother to San Francisco to audition for a film role.

The director, however, was more interested in Aldo and cast him in the 1951 film *Saturday's Hero*.

Later signed by Columbia Pictures he went on to star in a number of films that include the 1952 *The Acting Game*, the 1958 *The Naked and the Dead* and the 1985 *Evils of the Night*.

One particularly multi-talented and creative bearer of the Rae name was the British educator, writer, novelist and television panellist **Dr John Rae**.

Born in 1931, he was headmaster of Taunton School, in Somerset, from 1966 to 1970 and of Westminster School from 1970 to 1986.

His 1961 novel *The Custard Boys* was adapted for the 1962 film *Reach for Glory* – winner of a United Nations Award and adapted yet again for the 1979 film of the novel's original title.

On the board of the *Observer* newspaper from 1986 to 1993, he also appeared as a panellist on BBC radio and television programmes that include *Question Time* and *Any Questions*.

Further adding to his already impressive

curriculum vitae, in 1989 he became executive chairman of the Portman Group, which campaigns for the responsible consumption of alcohol.

His edited diaries, *The Old Boys' Network: A Headmaster's Diaries* were published three years after his death in 2006.